Previous page Eleanor Antin as Eleanora Antinova, 1980
From *Being Antinova*, 1983, Astro Artz Press
Documenting 30 days of living in the world as the black ballerina
Photo: Mary Swift

Foreword

The archaeology of history has presented us with histories of great men, great women, ordinary people, extraordinary events and precise moments welded to create a seamless narrative. Its practice tells us about our own society's desires and perspectives, through a dominant voice and a range of dissident opinions.

The heightened attention to the work of Eleanor Antin, its presentation in a major retrospective exhibition at the Los Angeles County Museum, Los Angeles in 1999 curated by Howard N. Fox and the development of this first exhibition for the United Kingdom reveals our perspectives at the turn of the twentieth century. Western belief in a simple, progressive dynamic has been lost in an age where the possibilities of social exclusion or inclusion depend on increasingly precarious economic security. The 1980s' ideology of individualism associated with booming economies has transmuted into a more anxious, introspective notion of self.

Eleanor Antin's work explores histories and identities that were deprecated at the time. She borrows from them and remakes them, fuses them with personal history and makes new connections with people from the past to explore contemporary issues. The incessantly hopeless yet moving efforts of a black ballerina, the clutter of suburban housewives in California, the fat on a woman's body; all are retrieved from the store room of repudiation and presented to us. Her work offers a sense of the fragility of our own realities. Witty, poignant and thoughtful, it requires the viewer to make some kind of connection beyond an aesthetic response to formally conceived objects; an imaginative response to a selection of found or store-bought objects that have cultural meanings. It is a narrative activity that requires willingness to make-believe from the viewer.

This first UK exhibition of the work of Eleanor Antin has been supported by the National Touring Programme of the Arts Council of England and will tour to Arnolfini in Bristol and Manchester Cornerhouse. We are grateful to the staff of all three organisations for their expertise in the development of this exhibition. We would like to thank the lenders to this exhibition who have so generously agreed to share their works by Eleanor Antin with a British audience: Ronald Feldman Fine Arts New York, Sabine Eckmann, Curator of the Washington University Gallery of Art, St. Louis, Marcia Goodman, the Los Angeles County Museum of Art, and Marc Nochella. We would like to acknowledge William Rowe and the in-kind support at Mainframe who have made it possible to include real time streaming in the exhibition itself rather than just in its title. Catherine Elwes, Howard N. Fox, Martha Rosler and Rachael Thomas have all contributed elegant and perceptive essays to this catalogue and we are grateful to them.

Above all, we would like to thank Eleanor Antin for the insights and energy with which she has endowed this exhibition. We hope that this first introduction to her work for British audiences will lead to other initiatives that involve an artist who continues to make work that adds resonance to our own lives.

Sarah Shalgosky
Curator, Mead Gallery

opposite
Eleanor Antin, *Love's Shadow* from *Loves of a Ballerina*,
From the *Archives of Modern Art*. Video tape 18 ½ minutes, black and white, 1987
Courtesy of Electronic Arts Intermix, New York. Photo by Becky Cohen

following pages
Eleanor Antin, detail from: *CARVING: A Traditional Sculpture* 1972
The piece consists of 148 photographs depicting 37 days of a weight loss of 11 pounds.
Exhibition copy, original at The Art Institute of Chicago, Twentieth Century Discretionary Fund, 1996. © Eleanor Antin

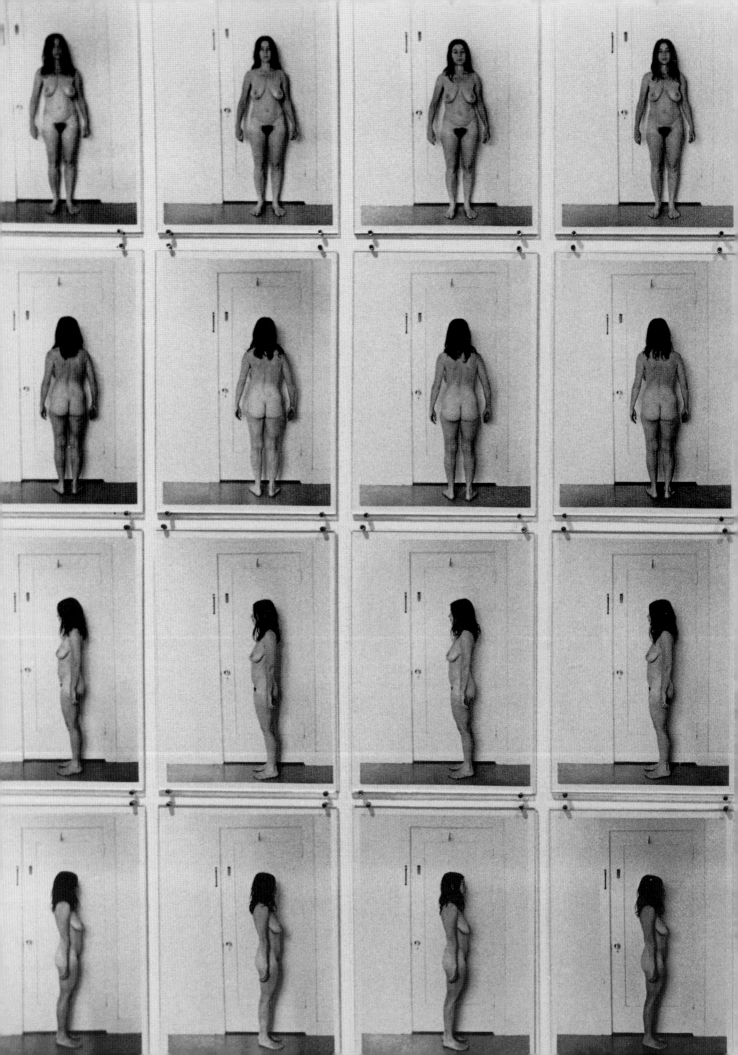

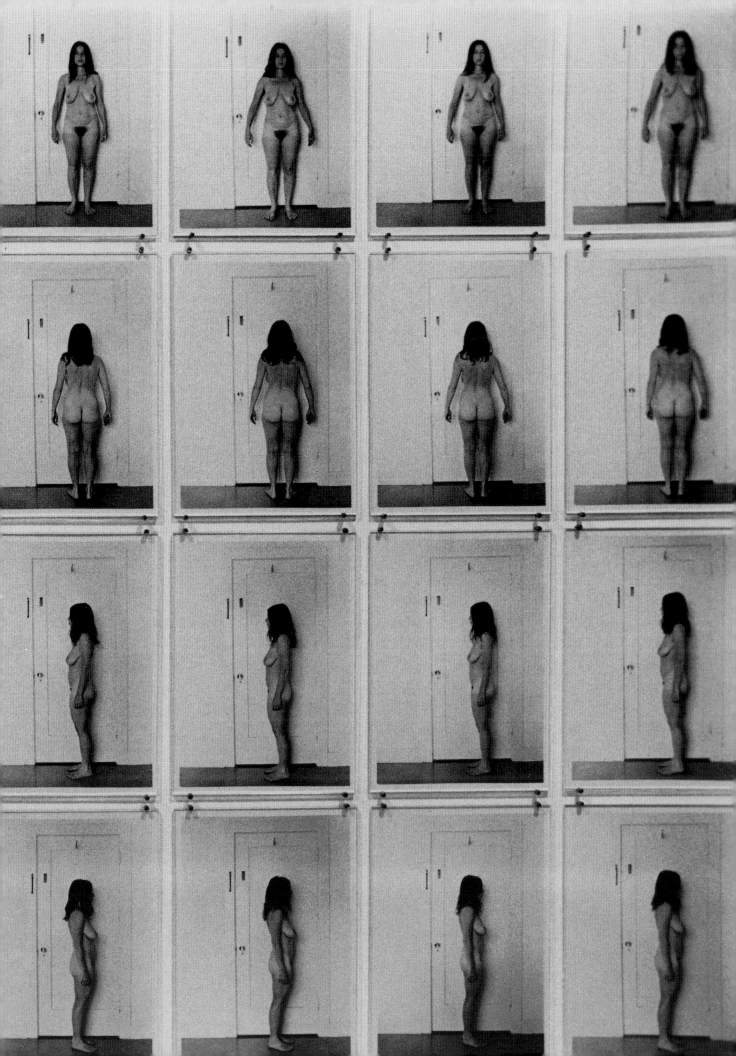

Eleanor Antin: Real Time Streaming

From my past life I gladly borrow,
I am who I was, who I am I will be.
There is no yesterday nor tomorrow
but only today forever for me.
Miguel de Unamuno, 'Last Poems'.[1]

Perhaps the fascination of storytelling lies in its potential to reanimate and resuscitate history. *Eleanor Antin: Real Time Streaming* explores the role of narratives, of representing life, literally many lives as she moves between personas past and present, both real and imagined to reflect and illuminate our world. Traditional narratives unfold in time, but Antin regards time 'as an epoch and genre rather than as an unfolding process'.[2]

Antin presents us with an alternative vision of historical time, one that emphasises its particularities, its characteristics whether they are political, aesthetic, sociological, or whether they are spectacular or perhaps quite banal. Antin disrupts historical time by questioning the chronological progression and factual authenticity of history, and does not regard it as sacred. It is as if she picks and chooses at will from the repository of history. Hers is a moving historical picture, one that is living – animated even, it is not a vision so hopelessly separated from the present, something so bygone that it seems somehow out of date, irrelevant to those living in *this* hour. It is a perception that shakes our temporal consciousness. Time need not necessarily pass from one moment to the next; it is possible for one moment to linger, to come back again and again as if it had never passed. That self-same moment, that winding tract of time, may also have countless interpretations.

But the essentially slippery, transformational nature of Antin's vision of time is also a consequence of the way she inserts herself as a contemporary being into seemingly remote historical periods and geographical spaces. She does this by appropriating different media and generic forms, fusing elements borrowed from a wide variety of possibilities, expressionist films, anonymous Victorian sepia photographs, to throwaway consumer junk. It is not entirely clear whether inserting herself into these historical roles and situations brings the present into the past or the past into the present. There is always, even in the midst of outlandishly comic events, a disturbing tension in her work, which mirrors the post-modern angst of the late 20th and early 21st centuries.

The exhibition title, *Real Time Streaming*, is taken from the increasingly familiar world of information technology; it refers to a digital process that transmits live events as a stream of images that can be watched by anyone with access to a computer. In this way people, wherever they are, are able to watch events synchronously as if they were all physically present. It enables computer users to glimpse another moment unfolding in some other place; it provides an alternate perspective at a touch of a button. *Real Time Streaming* defies the limitations of physicality, of 'being there'. It dislocates all voices. With a click it picks up a variety of fragmented worlds which seem to be powerfully present, as they become completely unreal. On many levels this exhibition questions the many representations of reality we are forced to live with in the post-modern world. Can reality, therefore be defined by the clothes we wear, the food we eat, the consumer goods we buy? By locating real time and real life in the every day we can look at how Antin's diverse simulacra of reality becomes difficult to categorise with one easy phrase or label. If no description exists for what she is doing then it is because she is in constant flux, moving in and out of genres, evading categories and limitations all the while – for this, she is to be applauded. She stretches boundaries and refuses to be contained. Her work is sometimes textual, sometimes sculptural, often using valueless objects – paper dolls, consumer junk – her work frequently moves into performance using video, film and other multi-media technologies to her advantage. Her live installations have pioneered the development of conceptual performance by linking elements of escapist drama, historical fictions and dark humour to explore contemporary themes with a certain freshness, with greater vitality. There are recurring elements that run through her work, ideas of identity, of role playing, whether they are historically located or situated in the present.

The exhibition investigates Antin's polymorphous work and employs a multitude of voices as she examines the nature of the social roles played by her created characters. She uses a wide variety of media to engage with a number of socio-political issues, moving freely from such disparate elements as simulated mid 19th century sepia photographs, to mid 20th century cinema montage storyboards. Even when her stories and installations are at their most absurd she always shows us that that we can never be completely removed from reality. In raiding life for art, she exploited rather than suppressed her literary and theatrical styles. Antin's practice is similar to that of an archaeologist, who uncovers and documents history, while at the same time having to invent the narratives that connect the isolated ruin fragments she has found. So far her findings are never static and her conclusions retain future transformations and narrative possibilities.

Born in Manhattan in 1935, Antin worked as an actor, a poet and an artist in the vigorous ferment of the New York Art world during the late 50s and throughout the 60s. This was a time when art was opening up to the world of everyday life in a storm of creative invention by pop artists, early minimalist and conceptual performance sculptors and dancers and the, even then, little known but radical movement known as Fluxus. Fluxus aimed to release the individual from all inhibitions whether they were physical, psychological or political.[3] It was disruptive, polemical, and anti-authoritarian. What appealed to Antin about Fluxus, was that there were no barriers, no distinction between art and life, they were both equally fluid and equally aestheticised. Antin also incorporated John Cage's and Marcel Duchamp's desire to consider life as theatre. By this, Cage included the sounds and silences of modern life and Duchamp sought to include objects and actions. This made the spectator not only more aware of him/herself but also of the surrounding world as well. The political turmoil of the anti-war movement led to the experimental liberation movements of feminism, gay liberation, black power, as real world energy became central to the radical art of the 70s. Artists opened an arena that went beyond the restrictions and limitations of paintings and discrete sculptures in 'white cube' galleries; they broke free of this confined space by staging dance, performance, installations and readings in the galleries and on the streets. By this time however, Antin was already bringing her avant-garde sensibility to southern California where she still lives. 'Everything here was open and up for grabs…Here in San Diego, we have the ocean on the west, the desert to the east, Hollywood's up north and Mexico's down south. How can you miss?" asks Antin.

The works featured in *Real Time Streaming* share this sense of theatrical presence as Antin manipulates the boundaries between daily life and art. One such work is the *Blood of a Poet Box*, 1965-8, for which she collected and preserved the blood of one hundred poets on glass microscope slides among them John Ashberry, David Antin, John Cage, Allen Ginsberg and Jerome Rothenberg. This work is an homage to the Jean Cocteau's film Le Sang d'un Poète of 1930. The *Blood of a Poet Box* works on many levels echoing Joseph Cornell and Marcel Duchamp with its conceptual and surreal sense of subject matter and its deadpan irony. For Antin, art has always been a form of investigation that reforms culture, making visible that which has been rendered invisible. Howard N. Fox, the Curator of Modern and Contemporary Art at the Los Angeles County Museum of Art, says of this work 'It implies a celebration of and a regard for life in its suggestion of human mortality. The piece is engaged in its social and cultural milieu'.[4] The work can also be seen as a metaphor 'lifeblood of art itself, ironically clinical (and bodiless)' but the title reflects the Victorian romantic *ideal* of the blood of a poet. The physical trace is the evidence.[5]

The exhibition also shows us the wide variety of genres and narratives out of which she makes her art. The well-known *100 Boots* and the mail art *Adventures of a 100 Boots, 1971-3,* is a fiction depicting the photographic adventures of 100 black rubber boots, who during the two and a half years of their mail distribution were sent to over a thousand artists, writers and musicians around the globe. The fifty-one postcards could be read as a photographic road movie, featuring the actual journey of 100 Boots who travel America from the Pacific Ocean to their final destination, New York's Museum of Modern Art, where on arrival they move into a crash pad built especially for them and become the focus of an exhibition. The witty, personification of the Boots as sort of 'Beat Heroes' is characteristic of Antin's deadpan humour. Similarly *Carving: A Traditional Sculpture, 1972*, is a sly deadpan photographic presentation of her weight loss over a 36 day period as she 'transformed' and 'internally carved' herself, into an 'ideal' self. *Carving: A Traditional Sculpture* also addresses feminist issues relaying representations of the body within the particular cultural context that has shaped the ideal of feminine beauty.

She draws upon familiar experiences by focusing on relationships and social systems, often as they affect women. This can been seen in early pieces such as *California Lives*, 1969, and *Portraits of Eight New York Women, 1970*. When Antin moved to Southern California she was inspired by the *Sears* catalogue for many of the objects in *California Lives* which were described in 1969, by the critic Amy Goldwin as 'Post-perceptual portraits'[6]. Using the cheap consumer goods sold in the Sears catalogue – electric razors, hair-rollers, TV trays, a ladder, to invent an iconic assortment of fictional and real people, all recognisable Californian types. Antin creates a gritty picture of old Southern California on the verge of being swept away by shopping malls and highways. This contribution to the emerging feminist discourse can also be seen in the *Portraits* of *Eight New York Women* who were in fact real and important figures of the New York art world, such as the visual and performance artist, Carolee Schneeman and the choreographer and dancer (since turned film-maker), Yvonne Rainer. By using this distinct approach to biography and later autobiography within her works, Antin does not avoid the issues of the day. She comments on the social and political position of women in the 70s and contributes to the feminist debate. Her approach is also satirical and witty, as importantly these two works were being produced at the same time that the American minimalist sculptor Donald Judd was producing stainless steel or painted iron boxes, set side by side, without narrative or emotional overtones. Unlike Judd, Antin moves between what is real and what is theatrical, encouraging the suspension of disbelief, and appealing to a subversive kind of humour.

As a theatrical device, Antin used masquerade in her performances. Masquerade was a vehicle employed by many feminist artists including Martha Wilson and Adrian Piper. Later masquerade also formed the foundation for Cindy Sherman's photographs beginning with the self- portraits series the *Untitled Film Stills,* where in the photograph Sherman created a tense, filmic type atmosphere. Yet Antin goes beyond the one liner. She breathes life into her characters as she creates, and recreates their ongoing worlds, challenging histories and disturbing more traditional modes of perceptions. In the persona of the King in *The King of Solana Beach, 1972-75,* Antin walked through the streets of San Diego with a large black hat, false beard and moustache and greeted all her 'bemused' subjects. The King is then seen in a series of photographs drinking beer with teenagers or queuing for money at a bank. If we compare Antin's *King of Solana Beach* with Adrian Piper's early photographic work *Mythic Being, 1972-5*, both works being done independently during the same period in different parts of the U.S., Antin on the West Coast and Piper on the East Coast, where Piper disguised herself as the androgynous, racially inconclusive man dressed in 70s flares, Jackie O sunglasses, and a big Afro wig with a Zappa -like moustache. Piper like Antin crossed boundaries of race and gender, by documenting a series of public performances and 'confusing' fact and fiction. This is done by Piper inserting autobiographical journal writings into her photographs of the *Mythic Being*. Both Antin and Piper were 'part of a small number of artists who placed a social critique into a broad conceptual framework, and used elements such as performance and photography to demonstrate that identity itself is bound up in performance and its representation'.[7]

In the personality obsessed art of the late twentieth century, Antin's personas are refreshing, as the fabrication and slightly not-quite authentic feel jars our consciousness. Antin interjects doubt into the imagined actuality of the historical moment, both as a commentary upon history but also an art strategy. As Antin writes, 'Its not the real thing which suggests the real in art, it is the slight disparity, the unexpected even, that will give the appearance of truth'[8]. For three weeks in 1980 Antin lived in New York as her invented persona, Eleanora Antinova, the once celebrated, but now retired black ballerina of Diaghilev's Ballet Russe. By living this character, daily darkening her skin colour and giving public performances in character, Antin engaged several contemporary issues of representation, identity, ethnicity and gender. In an early work *Caught in the Act, 1973,* Antin contrast the truth of the still camera with that of the moving camera as the video documents the Photographic shoot of the Ballerina, in typical, classical poses *en pointe*s. Yet she can't hold the poses, without balancing herself by holding onto a broomstick offered by a sympathetic friend named 'help', she falls and stumbles; loses her footing, all she can do is pretend for a split second before she falls that she is a real ballerina. Since it is the still camera that captures these frozen moments, the photographs on the wall prove that she is 'a ballerina' even if the video disproves it at the same time. As in *Carving: A Traditional Sculpture* we see the difficulties and pressures of achieving and maintaining cultural ideas of feminine beauty. These issues can also be seen in the younger generation of British artists such as Tracey Emin, Gillian Wearing and Linder Sterling.

Tracey Emin constructs the persona of artist who confesses her every-day life by re-accounting its painful events, from which Emin draws upon her own experiences. Emin uses her voice, whether it is recorded on video, or appliquéd on to blankets; what we then have is a confession and exposure to the fragility of the self. If we compare *Caught in the Act, 1973* to the video work *'Why I never became a Dancer'*, by Emin, we see that both works represent the image of the inner struggle of the self. Emin's dancing is a defiant act to her ex-lovers in Margate. The video recalls (through Emin's voice-over) a past event when Emin was shouted off the dance floor by 'a gang of boys, most of whom I had sex with'. Emin then left Margate for London and never wanted to dance again. Both use humour to veil more serious concerns about the subjugation of individual. Both artists' works represent an inner struggle with the self through the body, for both works point to issues that are at once personal and political, individual and social. Both works use the device of humour to expose the absurdity of the situations. This device of using humour in performance work can also be seen in the work of British artists Gilbert and George. *Singing Sculpture*, 1969, is a typical example of their humorous work. Gilbert and George mime to an old record *Underneath the Arches* while wearing stiff formal suits, their faces and hands painted gold.

Despite the genuine comedy that can erupt at any moment, Antin's subjects are usually the dispossessed or doomed outsiders in society, as Antinova in the 'Loves of a Ballerina' (1986). This multi-media installation dramatises Antinova's later career as a fallen artist who tries to eke out a living performing in seedy theatres. Antinova's career has fallen from the gilded heights and now she is desperate for attention, starring in risqué black and white silent films. Therefore the theme of social inclusion is one that is close to her heart, but one that is always unattainable. For how could a black ballerina make it in the white ballet world of the early 20th century? Stubborn, talented, clever she keeps fighting for the place in the sun which her talents deserve. By inserting this fictitious ballerina into the historical Russian ballet, and by making us care about her, Antin is re-writing history to emphasise her point.

Nowhere is this more powerfully accentuated than in '*The Man without a World*' (1991), a 16mm black and white silent feature film. Jeffrey Skoller writes that 'it is a film of a film made to evoke an absence, as a means to "see" what is no longer there'.[9] Antin invents a new character 'Yevgeny Antinov', the long forgotten Polish Jew who supposedly directed the film (from the opening titles we are led to believe that the film has recently been rediscovered). Playing the role of 'Antinov', the forgotten filmmaker, Antin inserts herself into a creative historical 'icon', which questions the representations and veracity of historical film. Both the *context* and *presentation* of the work are crucial to its reception; the film seems neglected, as if the celluloid has been lost for decades. By doing this, she conjures up an extinct world, one that blurs historical accuracy by mixing both fact and fiction. The film was inspired by the artist's desire to explore her Jewish past. Antin creates a 'fiction' and transforms it into an historical 'artefact'. Perhaps one of the most interesting aspects of the film is the way it opens other possibilities for our understanding of history, and its very personal memories. 'I have a head full of Ghosts', Antin laments, which brings to mind something of Baudelaire when he wrote:

'Old neighbourhoods – all allegory now – Old recollections weigh me down like rocks'.[10]

Memory according to the philosopher Ian Hacking, began to take over the role and popular concept of the soul, 'People were what they remembered, but importantly they also could be understood to be what they had forgotten'. Thus Antin skilfully shows that her work is an on-going practice of memories, both real and fictitious, and rather than being merely a collection of individual works, each work informs the next, in a ceaseless, streaming conversation.

Antin's work is symptomatic of an age in which a multitude of voices was striving to have their stories told and narratives heard, as they fought against the age old repressive silence. A sense of the necessity of narrative underlies her work, it unfolds stories of multiple personas and alter egos that make their claim amongst the limitations of time and space. 'The usual aids to self-definition', she remarks, 'are merely tyrannical limitations upon my freedom of choice'.[11] Antin brackets these claims with an ironic, vernacular, low-tech approach. 'Real Time Streaming' therefore challenges the slick, sanitised portrayals of contemporary lifestyles that seem to fixate so much of popular culture. Her sophisticated exploitation of media allows her to replicate the low-tech appearance and imperfections of antiquated technologies of old film, as well as their haunting glamour. This constitutes a radical contrast with the technically perfect (and sterile) output of popular film and television, such as the visually slick films *TimeCode* or *Memento*. Our current media is dominated by self-help programmes such as *Home Front* and *How to Cook*, in which we are shown how to attain the sophisticated, homogeneous, *ideal* lifestyle in an afternoon; one which has no mess, no chaos and is *always* complete perfection. Yet, real life is not like television, for reality is a fictional representation open to many simulacra's of real life, all illogical and uncertain. Real Time Streaming presents the often distressing, frequently funny, evidence of real life without covering up our very human emotions and reactions. As the world gauges success by money, fashion and status, Antin questions the primacy of these value systems. Hers is a voice that has not been marginalised; in fact it has grown stronger, as it presides over the collision of past and present histories. Her narratives are indubitably uncomfortable. Antin recognises that pathos and failure play crucial roles in our lives and she constantly weaves these strands together in unexpected and often spectacular ways. Antin's work intervenes and disturbs the dominant voice-over of history. Her vignettes give us insight into the complexities and contradictions of life, into the imperfect beauty of our illogical, irrational lives. Through Antin's work there is a hope that we can all lose, then finally find ourselves, anew.

Rachael Thomas, Assistant Curator

January 2001

1   Miguel de Unamuno, 'The Last Poems of Miguel de Unamuno' (1974: 115).
2   Kim Levin. 'Beyond Modernism' (1988: 107).
3   Herbert Read, 'History of Modern Painting' (1974: 310).
4   Howard Fox, 'Eleanor Antin' (1999). A retrospective catalogue, Los Angeles County Museum of Art.
5   Henry Sayre, 'Ghost Stories' (1996). Southeastern Centre for Contemporary Art, U.S.A.
6   Amy Goldin, The Post Perceptual Portrait, Art in America, Jan/Feb 1975
7   Frazer Ward, Adrian Piper, Frieze, pg 80 1998.
8   Kim Levin, 'Beyond Modernism' (1988: 113).
9   Jeffrey Skoller, 'The Man Without a World' (1995) Film Quarterly 49.
10 Charles Baudelaire, 'The Swan' in 'Complete Poems' (1997: 227).
11 Howard Fox, 'Eleanor Antin' (1999). A retrospective catalogue, Los Angeles County Museum of Art.

following pages
The Gentleman's Game is the Ladies Gain from *The Angels of Mercy.* 1977
Courtesy of the Whitney Museum of American Art, New York © Eleanor Antin

Eleanor Antin, 'Eleanora Antinova at the Metropolitan Museum of Art'
Photo by Mary Swift

Eleanor Antin: A Petite Disquisition

In the natural history of modern artists' careers, especially those who engage prevailing interests of the prevailing avant garde, it is common for artists to endure periods of prominence and eclipse and rediscovery. Eleanor Antin - a legendary figure in the emergence of conceptual, performance, video, and installation art, and a forerunner in the advent of feminist art - is currently enjoying something of a renaissance. Yet I believe it is not because of a critical rehabilitation or a creative comeback. Antin, after all, had never disappeared from the scene; for more than three decades she has been actively and continually at work. Indeed, virtually everything that she has created - from her early postal art to her films, filmic installations, and audio pieces - has been shown in museums and galleries either in the United States or internationally. I can think of no other artist whose entire oeuvre has been publicly exhibited at one time or another.

But why the recent resurgence of interest surrounding Antin? When I organized a retrospective exhibition of Antin at the Los Angeles County Museum of Art in 1999, I discovered that a whole generation of upcoming artists and critics was having its first contact with her art. Young doctoral students were writing their dissertations on Antin's pioneering work in video and conceptual art dating from a time before there was even a critical vocabulary in place to describe them as such. Young artists were looking anew at narrative modes and autobiographical art forms, and they found in Antin's history a complex exemplar of the rich possibilities of these modes. Cultural historians were writing about Antin's contribution to the impetus for the women's art movement. And savvy young collectors and contemporary curators at some major museums were finally getting around to an opportunity that had eluded their predecessors: acquiring her art works, nearly all of which went unsold even while they were widely exhibited and critically acclaimed. Antin's "renaissance" is really less a critical development within her own career than a new awakening by a younger generation and the well-earned appreciation of her own generation and their near contemporaries.

Even though Antin's art reflects the artistic, political, social, and cultural concerns of the times when it was created, the fact is she has always worked somewhat anachronistically, out of synch with the rest of the art world. For example, Antin was staging costume dramas while others were bulldozing earth or hoisting vast slabs or Cor-Ten steel into precarious balancing acts. She was acting out the invented personal histories of her fictional other "selves" - a king, a nurse, a ballerina - at the same time that other more dominant artists were drawing grids or stain-painting shaped canvases. She was making counterfeit Victorian-era photographs when other photographers were documenting teenage heroin addicts. She was producing convincing simulacra of vintage silent movies when other artists were beginning to look at digital technologies.

Yet, if her production seems to be out of kilter with its time, her art also has a poetic timelessness evoked by enduring and perennial themes that loom powerful in the human imagination. In the height of the modern age, Antin maintains a yearning for the ideal of an exalted, transcendent, high, and perhaps grand art that has the power to hold and claim and change peoples' lives. It is a dream oddly told through the trappings of popular culture and with the charms of a lyrical make-believe, a child-like inventiveness, and an unrequited wishing-it-were-so. Throughout her oeuvre, Antin presents herself consistently and finally as an idealist and an existentialist, one who lives a dear and hopeful life-in-art while harboring the steel-cold knowledge that death is its real and lasting result. End, and beginning, of disquisition.

Howard N. Fox
Curator of Modern and Contemporary Art, Los Angeles County Museum of Art

Self-portrait of the artist as...
Eleanor Antin

Eleanor Antin has rightly attained iconic status in the pantheon of American conceptual and feminist art of the I970s. She was one of the first artists to interrogate the traditional limitations of her gender by re-inventing herself in a rich cast of characters including The King, The Nurse and the Black Ballerina, Eleanora Antinova, a symbol of the artist's creative self. Through an investigation of gender she was able to raise further issues of race, religion, displacement and ecology. It is often said that the archetypal personae she created allowed her imaginatively to experience aspects of life, past and present to which she would not otherwise have gained access in her condition as a contemporary white woman. But she went beyond the initial urgency of a Utopian feminism and embraced darker visions. Many of her impersonations took her into lives that reflect the tragedy of the human condition. She herself asked the question, 'Isn't defeat built into the world, as basic as carbon?' [1]

Within all her alter egos, Antin confirmed the equivocal and mutable nature of identity as well as the power of women to transform their lives in a new world of political and cultural equality emerging in the 1960s. Whether appropriating the putative power of a King or the poignancy of a fading ballerina, Antin steps out of her own life, or perhaps sideways into an imagined reality reworked within the dramatic license of a performed present. Knowing her work only as necessarily fictive recreations in the form of documentation, I read these personae less as speculative departures from Antin's actual life and more as expressions of her evolving experiences as a woman, as an artist and a Jewish American with eastern European roots. Although Antin asserts that her work represents the lives she has chosen not to live, these characters nonetheless embody the images she has elected to create and as such they document the evolution of her ideas, her politics, her moral positions and her persistent investigations of identity.

Taken as a whole, these myriad personalities are the shifting fragments that make up a life-long self-portrait of the artist as Eleanor Antin. The power of the King is Antin's creative impulse unleashed in the political world. His idealism her own, his defeat her inability to deny the realities of western capitalism. The Nurse tells us that Antin has a frivolous side and Eleanor Nightingale betrays a deeply concerned and unfashionable humanism. As she grows older, Antin explores her roots in the dramatic recreation of pre-war shtetl life in Poland. To borrow the life as art anthem of the 1970s, Antin's work is not reducible to a series of fictions, but constitutes a creative document of her life. As any one of her characters and as a woman artist, the marginal position she inhabits is not a tragedy, but a necessarily detached vantage point from which she may create. In this way she can explore her histories, comment on what she finds and construct her ongoing self-portrait with what she describes as the "..delicious feeling of removal and being at the same time."[2] We may well need reminding that in the I970s, Eleanor Antin's insistence that the creative imagination of a woman should be recognised as the proper concern of art was radical both politically and culturally in a persistently patriarchal world.

Antin is less well known in this country than she is in her native America. Her delicious ability to trip lightly through European history stealing characters as she went might have been regarded as over-theatrical and too subjective for the academic imperatives of '70s feminism in England. There would have been more sympathy for her early conceptual exercises in pseudo-scientific documentation of life. It wasn't until the late '70s that British performance artists themselves began exploring aspects of their psyche in other guises: Rose

Finn-Kelcey inhabited the spirit of a magpie, Sylvia Zyranek lived an almost continuous parody of an English housewife and Jo Spence photographed herself impersonating all the femininities she 'missed' by becoming an artist. But these works were less well known than the output of more academic feminists who dismissed performance art as doomed to replicate the sexual objectification of women by presenting the spectacle of the artist's body for the gratification of a male audience.

Ostensibly, younger British women have now thrown out feminist theory, in all its forms. And yet, in recent years, we have seen Sarah Lucas joining Antin and the rich history of cross-dressing by parodying the more extreme manifestations of loutish masculinity. But where Lucas is busy unsettling the fixity of gender through a play of surfaces, Antin searched out in her male disguise the essence of what she calls her "political self".[3] The declared political dimension is what separates these two artists' work and indeed the two generations of women artists they represent.

In 1995, the British artist Gillian Wearing performed *Homage to the woman* with the bandaged face who I saw yesterday down the Walworth Road. Sharing Eleanor Antin's fascination for the damaged and the dispossessed, Wearing bandaged her own face and video recorded a parallel journey down the Walworth road. If we read this work as an unintentional homage to Antin, Wearing might be anticipating the day when contemporary women artists link their present to our feminist past. Perhaps some intrepid student will take Antin herself as an iconic alter ego and through their conjoined journeys we will listen in on another life and learn how the next generation view gender, race, and the future of the planet.

Catherine Elwes
January 2001

1   Eleanor Antin speaking to Howard N. Fox in the catalogue Eleanor Antin,
     Los Angeles County Museum of Art, 1999
2   Ibid.
3   Ibid.

Previous page
Eleanora Antinova, Recollections of my Life with Diaghilev, (performance), 1980
Courtesy of Ronald Feldman Fine Arts Gallery, New York

Opposite
Eleanor Antin, *Blood of a Poet Box, 1965-68*, (with the materials used in its making).
Photo by Peter Moore

Exiles in Paradise

IF WE MET in the tailing-down, scaling- down, dissipating bohemia of New York City mid-1960s, there was just enough generational space between us for Eleanor Antin and David Antin to act as guides of sorts as well as friends. (And Diane and Jerry Rothenberg, co-conspirators in cheaply elegant poetry publishing.) We share continuity with avant-garde New York of the late 1950s through 1960s, the loosely formed society of disaffected malcontent geniuses chewing through art and intellectual culture. (Have you heard of bohemia? It was really there then, though sinking Atlantis-like into whatever came later--success I suppose? or maybe something else.)

Children of immigrants and patrician renegades, passionately fleeing Yiddish and other languages snatching at the hems of American English, threading through political cultures bringing to mind Weegee's Critic, yentas and rude guys in impossible clothes moved to downtown hovels, from the Bronx, Brooklyn, the Lower East Side, from City and Hunter and Brooklyn College or bounced out of tonier long-lineage private schools, actresses poets dancers writers filmmakers painters, away from polite-culture airconditioned-nightmares, in favor of Beckett Ionesco Robert Frank Bataille de Sade, Godard Resnais Chabrol Antonioni Rossellini, Dahlberg Burroughs, Cendrars, Stein, Artaud and The Living Theatre, Williams the beats Ginsberg Corso sweet Ferlinghetti, Duncan Creeley Bly (the Roberts), Blackburn (an early casualty) Hollo Finley the Black Mountain people (got new religion), Cage, Cunningham, Rochelle Owens Wakoski di Prima Levertov, La Monte Young, Glass, Corner, Kupferberg & the Fuggs, Ed Sanders (bookstore and *Fuck You*, a Magazine of the Arts.)...Fluxus Maciunas Brecht Ono, Schneeman's Meat Joy Rainer Tharp, Morris (what you see is what you see); Oldenburg Warhol Cale Nico Malanga Morrisey Candy Darling. And against the criminal wars, and for the Angry arts. Oh, and...hey! little dope except among the younger set!

Bohemia, neither heaven nor hell... in 1965 bohemia we could see (as recorded in *Pull My Daisy*) that women were mostly *ancillary*. On my birthday just before my son's birth(day) an important (woman) poet wrote on a big beautiful art book she brought to my party, May you always be in the company of poets... Ellie, having recently had her own baby, says: How about BEING a poet? Her *Blood of a Poet*, deliciously vampirish, vengeful, blood of the poets, those important men and some high-horse ladies - Ellie could administer tiny painful jabs to obtain a magic trace (look forward to the Nurse) .... genius is ascribed to (or claimed by) people who remain no more than flesh. And she had a system, or anyway a suitcase, a collection box. A machine to generate art, she always said, was valuable, acknowledging with some regret not having one. (I was learning that art was not natural.) Jackson Maclow, Ellie says, made a system, an aleatory system to defuse sentimentality. I got it (not a system, the idea). It is better to think things through than to see the dead minds of your generation bearded with moss and in garments green (no to Ginsberg, they opined; too hot). Ellie's systems were "off" systems, riffs that showed up the melody for its creaky pretensions and privileges rotting the insides. Why be legal? Oh, and by the way, collage is the art of the twentieth century. And from the collage, the fragment, even if cleverly ordered in grids and series.

IF WE SAT with our 1967 babies on the Promenade in Brooklyn Heights, it was not because that was the end, that view toward Manhattan. We looked further than the Bronx, we sat, all night after all night, at the Antins' kitchen table, arguing art and poetics, plays and politics, Ellie, David and I and my partner, and what didn't I learn? I learned that the rules of the game were precisely what made the art system (new idea) vulnerable because the rules were brittle. You, she said, are always the colonizer or the colonized (shades of Memmi? and Fanon?)

Meanwhile, being on the outside was still to be somewhere, that fine aforementioned place full of fine people and the ghosts of the likes of (say) yeats pound joyce stein and the witty dada army.

IF WE MOVED to San Diego California—what was that about? adventure, a real job—it didn't mean leaving all behind. Six months after the Antins, we moved there too, to scholarship heaven in the linguistics area. Promised paradise California sunshine (cold wet foggy too). Yes, paradise, but as Ellie complained, it tried to seem so, so white... except, she noted, it wasn't. We all missed the city mix as we moved from city to enclave.... so sixties. Soon enough I was living alone with my son and then I became a graduate student. My ideas and plans were tested there at the new kitchen table or under a tree burdened with oranges, and we disagreed mightily as we agreed on so much.

Now there was the (powerful, absorbing) women's movement alongside (with and against) the antiwar movement and for civil rights (now black power). Ellie and I joined/formed a group with other women younger and older; we met talked drew wandered and did free-floating performances. Performance was a wide invention of the Southern California women's movement, especially in LA. They did it, we did it even some in New York did it. (Soon even a man or two did it.) Ellie carried it to a new moment: the infusion of art history and melodrama into a persona-driven form, from the point of view of the impudent, because excluded (woman), Critic. Ellie was also working with video, a new medium we knew of from elsewhere, with possibilities of production and more to the point distribution better than film (which like most we dreamed of, getting as far as plots plans and still photography). She drew my attention to it also.

Soon Charlie Cox, the man running the video studio in the Med School basement, offers to teach David (who after all was faculty) and 5 or 6 students how to do it ourselves. We take him up. So I make video too. My friends in my other working group (did I mention them?), the motley UCSD photographers, well, one or two of them learn too. Ellie and I hang out. She develops her brilliant strategies (how about post-card art for starters--where did I get my mailing list?) Those boots march. in effect, past my door. I am happy to be in Ellie's shameless and elegant Civil War extravaganzas, a character (sometimes a cardboard cutout) in various costume dramas.

Art is the main game, Ellie says, everyone else is some kind of a civilian.

Years pass. And I graduated, did some teaching and meanwhile Ellie joins the faculty. Bohemia and assorted types reshape academe. And I moved away.

Ellie, notice, for a decade and more provided strategic moves, friendship (but please give her the credit of not assuming she was all that good-tempered!), nurturance, spaghetti, a model of theatical presence, syncretism, brash inventiveness, brilliance passion absurdity and a general all around insubordination that resonate with me still. And she continues. And she gets better. And her reach is wider. (And her movies are wonderful too.) Vive le roi! ...because who says a king has to be a man, with or without a head?

Martha Rosler

Previous pages
Eleanor Antin, *100 Boots on the Job*, 1972.
Signal Hill, California, February 15th 1972, 12:15pm. Courtesy of Ronald Feldman, Fine Arts Gallery, New York

Opposite above
Eleanor Antin, *100 BOOTS Turn the Corner*, 1972.
Courtesy of Ronald Feldman, Fine Arts Gallery, New York

Opposite middle
Eleanor Antin, *100 BOOTS on the Ferry*
Upper Harbour, New York City, May 16th, 1973, 11.20am.
Courtesy of Ronald Feldman, Fine Arts Gallery, New York

Opposite below
Eleanor Antin, *100 BOOTS on the Way to Church*, 1971-73.
Courtesy of Ronald Feldman, Fine Arts Gallery, New York

Above
Namoi Dash *from Portraits of Eight New York Women*, 1970
(Towel bar, towel, box of kitty litter, stockings, shower cap)
Photo: Peter Moore.

opposite and above

Eleanor Antin as the King, 1972.
Courtesy of Washington University Gallery of Art, St Louis. University purchase, art acquisition fund and Charles H. Yalem Art Fund 2000

opposite and above
Eleanor Antin as *The King of Solana Beach* 1974/5
Courtesy of Washington University Gallery of Art, St Louis. University purchase, art acquisition fund and Charles H. Yalem Art Fund 2000

opposite
Eleanor Antin in *The Little Match Girl Ballet 1975*
Courtesy Electronic Art Intermix, New York

above
Eleanor Antin in *The Ballerina and the Bum 1974*
Courtesy Electronic Art Intermix, New York

above
Eleanor Antin in *Escape* from live performance, 1975,
Palace of the Legion of Honour, San Francisco.

opposite
Eleanor Antin in *The Adventures of A Nurse*, 1976
Courtesy Electronic Art Intermix, New York

Installation view from *The Nurse and the Highjackers*, 1977
Video courtesy of Electronic Arts Intermix, installation Eleanor Antin.

Photo still from *The Last Night of Rasputin*, 1989
Courtesy Milestone Film and Video, New York, installation Eleanor Antin.

above
Installation view, Eleanor Antin from *Loves of a Ballerina,* 1986,
From the *Archives of Modern Art* Videotape, B&W, 1987
Courtesy of Eleanor Antin

opposite
Installation view from the *Loves of a Ballerina,* 1986,
One of three pieces from the Loves of a Ballerina installation
Courtesy of Eleanor Antin

above
Installation view Eleanor Antin *The Loves of a Ballerina*, 1986
Courtesy Eleanor Antin

opposite
Eleanor Antin, from *Help! I'm in Seattle*, performance 1986.
Courtesy Eleanor Antin

following pages
Eleanor Antin as Eleanova Antinova, *5th Avenue*, October 1980, New York City
Photo by Mary Swift

The time is now.

Eleanor Antin

REPRESENTATION
Ronald Feldman Fine Arts, New York (Art)
Milestone Film & Video, New York (Film)
Electronic Arts Intermix, New York (Video)

BOOKS
1983   Being Antinova, Astro Artz Press,
        Los Angeles, CA. OUT OF PRINT
1995   Eleanor Antin Plays,
        Sun & Moon, Los Angeles, CA.
1999   100 Boots, Running Press, Phila., PA
1999   Eleanor Antin, by Howard Fox,
        Los Angeles County Museum of Art
        & Fellows of Contemporary Art
2001   The Man Without a World,
        film script with pix of 1991 film,
        Green Integer, Sun & Moon Press,
        Los Angeles, CA.

30 SELECTED ONE-WOMAN EXHIBITIONS (out of 46)
1970   Gain Ground Gallery, New York
        Chelsea Hotel, New York
1971-73 United States Postal Distribution
        (through the mail), "100 Boots"
1972   Henri Gallery, Washington DC
1973   Museum of Modern Art, New York
1974   Everson Museum, Syracuse, New York
1975   Stefanotty Gallery, New York
1976   The Clocktower, New York,
1977   M.L. D'Arc Gallery, New York
        La Jolla Museum of Contemporary Art, CA.
        (now San Diego MOCA)
        Ronald Feldman Fine Arts Gallery, N.Y.
        Wadsworth Atheneum, Hartford, Connecticut
1978   Whitney Museum of American Art, New York
        Long Beach Museum of Art, CA.
        Los Angeles Institute of Contemporary Art
1979   Ronald Feldman Fine Arts Gallery, New York
1980   Ronald Feldman Fine Arts Gallery, New York
1981   Los Angeles Institute of Contemporary Art
1983   Ronald Feldman Fine Arts Gallery, New York
1986   Ronald Feldman Fine Arts Gallery, New York
1995   Ronald Feldman Fine Arts Gallery, New York
        Santa Monica Museum of Art, Los Angeles
        Craig Krull Gallery, Los Angeles
1997   Whitney Museum of American Art
1998   Ronald Feldman Fine Arts Gallery, New York
1999   Los Angeles County Museum of Art,
        Retrospective exhibition 1969-2000
        Washington University Gallery of Art, St. Louis, MO.
        Retrospective exhibition
2001   Mead Gallery, Warwick Arts Centre,
        University of Warwick, UK,
        "Eleanor Antin: Real Time Streaming"
        (retrospective), travel to Arnolfini Gallery,
        Bristol, UK and the Cornerhouse, Manchester, UK

Selected PERFORMANCES out of 75
Venice Biennale, Italy
Woman's Building, Los Angeles
Palace of Fine Arts, San Francisco
Palace of the Legion of Honour, San Francisco
American Theatre Association Convention, Los Angeles
Museum of Contemporary Art, Chicago
Contemporary Arts Museum, Houston, Texas
The Kitchen Center for New Music, Video, and Dance, NY
Santa Barbara Museum of Art, CA.
National Women's Caucus for Art, CAA., New Orleans
11th Annual International Sculpture Conference, Wash. D.C.
(Forum theatre)
Newport Harbor Art Museum, CA.
Los Angeles Institute of Contemporary Art
Contemporary Arts Museum, Houston, TX
LACE, Los Angele
Oklahoma City Museum of Fine Arts
Institute of Contemporary Art, Boston
Laguna Beach Museum of Art, CA.
Franklin Furnace, NY
Bowery Theatre, San Diego
Beyond Baroque, Los Angeles
MOCA Los Angeles
Whitney Museum, NY
Los Angeles County Museum of Art

FILM FESTIVALS AND SCREENINGS (selected list)
Berlin International Film Festival
USA Film Festival, Dallas
Flanders International Film Festival, Ghent, Belgium
11th Annual Jewish Film Festival, San Francisco
Festival of Jewish Cinema, Melbourne & Sydney, Australia
7th Jewish Film Festival, British Film Institute, London
Boston Jewish Film Festival
Women Directors, Women in Film and AFI, Los Angeles
Whitney Museum
Instituto de Estudios Norteamericanos, Barcelona
Portland Art Museum
Filmforum, Los Angeles
Pacific Film Archives, Berkeley
Principado de Asturias, Oviedo, Spain
National Gallery of Canada
Museum of Modern Art, Rio de Janeiro
Savassi Cineclub, Belo Horizonte, Brazil
Nabuco Foundation, Recife, Brazil
Image Farm, Hiroshima, Japan
Village East Cinemas, N.Y.
Honolulu Academy of Arts, Hawaii
Castro Theatre, San Francisco; Landmark Theatres, Berkeley, CA.
Laemmle Monica Plex, Los Angeles Harvard University
Baltimore Film Forum, Md.
Wexner Center for the Arts, Ohio; Hallwalls, N.Y.
Cinematheque, San Francisco

GROUP EXHIBITIONS
(Selected list from over 200 shows, all with catalogues)
1969   Dwan Gallery, New York, "Language 3"
1971   Museum of Modern Art of Buenos Aires,
        "Art Systems"
1974   Project '74, Cologne, Germany, "Video"
1975   Long Beach Museum, CA.,
        "Southland Video Anthology"
        Sao Paolo Biennale, Sao Paolo, Brazil,
        "Video Art U.S."
1976   Long Beach Museum, California,
        "Southland Video Anthology 2"
1977   Museum of Contemporary Art, Chicago,
        "Art of the Decade"
        Contemporary Arts Museum, Houston, Texas,
        "American Narrative/Story Art"
1978   Philadelphia Museum of Fine Arts,
        "Eight Artists"
1979   Hirshhorn Museum, Washington, D.C.,
        "Directions"
1981   Contemporary Arts Museum, Houston,
        "Other Realities: Installations for Performance"
1983   Museum of Modern Art, New York,
        "Video Art: A History," Part 2
1984   Hirshhorn Museum,
        "Content: A Contemporary Focus, 1974-84"
1988   International Center for Photography,
        New York, "Fabrications - Staged, Altered,
        and Appropriated Photographs," travelled to
        Carpenter Center, Harvard
1989   Whitney Museum, New York,
        "Biennial Exhibition,"
1989-90 Muenchner Kunstverein, Germany,
        "Constructed Realities," (travelled)
1992   Laguna Art Museum, California,
        "Proof: Los Angeles Art and the Photograph,
        1960-1980," also Friends of Photography,
        Ansel Adams Center, San Francisco
1993   Jewish Museum,N.Y.,
        "From the Inside Out: Eight Contemporary Artists"
        Turner/Krull Galleries, Los Angeles,
        "Action, Performance and the Photograph" (travel)
1995   MOCA, Los Angeles,
        "1965-1975: Reconsidering the Object of Art"
1997   La Magasin Centre National d'art Contemporain,
        Grenoble, France,
        "Vraiment Feminisme et Art"
1998   Museum of Contemporary Art, Los Angeles,
        "Out of Actions: Between
        Performance and the Object, 1949-1979"
        (travel Vienna, Barcelona, Tokyo, Osaka)
1999   Whitney Museum, N.Y., "American Century"
        Queens Museum, N.Y.,
        "Global Conceptualism: Points of Origin,
        1950-1980"

2000   Generali Foundation, Vienna, Austria,
        "Dinge Die Wir Nicht Verstehen"
        ("Things We Don't Understand")
        Centro Cultural de Belem, Lisbon, Portugal,
        "Eleanor Antin/Harun Farocki (2 person)
        Galerie im Taxispalais, Munich, Germany,
        "Die Verletzte Diva" ("The Wounded Diva: Hysteria,
        Body, Technology in 20th Century Art")
        Nelson Atkins Museum, Kansas City, Kansas,
        "Tempis Fugit"
        Los Angeles County Museum of Art,
        "Made in California"
        LACMA LAB, Los Angeles County Museum of Art,
        "NOW"
        Museum of Modern Art, N.Y., "MOMA 2000"

ARTICLES, ESSAYS, REVIEWS, INTERVIEWS
(selected list from over 300 publications)
Lucy Lippard, Christopher Knight, Peter Frank, Arthur Danto, Cindy Nemser, Carol Duncan, John Russell, Peter Plagens, Jonathon Crary, Douglas Davis, Kim Levin, J. Hoberman, William Wilson, Moira Roth, Suzanne Muchnik, Sally Banes, Bonnie Marranca, Howard Fox, Michael Kimmelman, Arlene Raven, Robert Pincus-Witten, Lynn Zelevansky, Grace Glueck, Henry Sayre, Lisa Bloom, Laurence Alloway, Annette Insdorf, Leah Ollman, Susan Freudenheim, Kay Larson, Jacki Apple, Anne d'Harnancourt, Elizabeth Baker, A.D.Coleman, Vicki Goldberg.

In the N.Y.Times, LA Times, Art Forum, Art in America, Art News, Art International, Studio International, Flash Art, Arts Magazine, Interview Magazine, MS Magazine, Washington Post, Village Voice, Feminist Studies,The Nation, Art Week, Vogue, Premiere, Variety, Film Quarterly, Chrysalis, Wall Street Journal, Camera Austria, Performance Arts Journal, etc.

RECENT AWARDS
Guggenheim, 1997
National Foundation for Jewish Culture Media Award, 1998

SELECTED PUBLIC COLLECTIONS
Whitney Museum; Museum of Modern Art, N.Y
Art Institute of Chicago; Jewish Museum,N.Y.
Museum of Contemporary Art, San Diego
Museum of Modern Art, San Francisco
Wadsworth Atheneum, Hartford, Conn.
Los Angeles County Museum of Art
The Washington University Gallery of Art, St. Louis

EMPLOYMENT
Professor of Visual Arts,University of California at San Diego,1975-present

List of Works

Selected Retrospective

1 Blood of a Poet Box, 1965-68
Wood box containing 100 glass slides of poets' blood specimens and specimen list 11 x 7 x 1 inches.

2 Here, from **Movie Boxes**, 1969-70
Photomontage and text in aluminium and glass case 37 x 25 x 3 inches.
Lent by Marcia Goodman

3 And, from **Movie Boxes** , 1969-70
Photomontage and text in aluminium and glass case 37 x 25 x 3 inches
Lent by Marcia Goodman

4 Coming, from **Movie Boxes**, 1969-70
Photomontage and text in aluminium and glass case 37 x 25 x 3 inches
Lent by Marcia Goodman, Encinitas, California

5 Jeanie, from **California Lives**, 1969
Replicated 1998
Folding TV snack table, melamine cup and saucer, plastic hair curler, king-size filter-tipped cigarette, matchbook and text panel
Dimensions variable

6 Molly Barnes, from **California Lives**, 1969
Replicated 1999
Acrylic bath mat, lady's electric razor, pills, talcum powder and text panel
Dimensions variable

7 The Murfins, from **California Lives**, 1969
Replicated 1999
Aluminium stepladder, trowel, can of adhesive, fresca can, faux brick tiles and text panel
Dimensions variable

8 Merrit, from **California Lives**, 1969
Replicated 1998
Gasoline can, bush hat with "peace" decal, metal comb and text panel
Dimensions variable

9 Naomi Dash, from **Portraits of Eight New York Women**, 1970
Replicated 1998
Chrome towel rack, bath towel, nylon stockings, shower cap, litter box with litter and text panel
Dimensions variable

10 Carolee Schneemann, from **Portraits of Eight New York Women**, 1970 Replicated 1998
Wood easel, mirror, jar of honey with honeycomb, crushed crimson velvet and text panel
Dimensions variable

10 Lynn Traiger, from **Portraits of Eight New York Women**, 1970
Replicated 1998
Wood door and jamb, leather key case with keys, straw doormat, glass milk bottle, plastic cottage cheese container, paper envelope, and text panel
Dimensions variable

12 The Red Bottle series, 1970
Typewritten paper mounted on panel
Five, each approximately 11 x 14 inches

13 100 BOOTS, 1971-73
Black and White picture postcards
Fifty-one postcards, each 4 x 7 inches
Exhibited with recipients' responses and other related ephemera
Courtesy of The Los Angeles County Museum of Art

14 100 BOOTS in Their Crash Pad, 1973
One hundred black rubber boots, wood door and jamb, porcelain sink mounted on wall, lightbulb on electrical wire,mattress, sheets, blankets, sleeping bags, radio with vintage 1973 music sound track, flooring, molding and wallpaper
Dimensions variable
Courtesy of The Los Angeles County Museum of Art

15 Representational Painting, 1971
Videotape (black-and-white, silent, thirty-eight minutes)
Courtesy of Electric Arts Intermix, New York

16 Library Science, 1971
Twelve black-and-white photographs,
each 12.125 x 8.125 inches
inches with accompanying Library of Congress catalogue cards, each 3 x 5 inches , library step stool, seven exhibition announcement cards, text panel, three explanatory sheets, library card
Dimensions variable

17 Domestic Peace, 1971-72
Handwritten text on graph paper and typewritten text and ink on paper.
Seventeen pages, each 8.5 x 11 inches

18 4 Transactions, 1972
Typewritten text and ink on paper.
Four pages, each 11 x 8 inches

19 Renunciations, 1972
Typewritten text on paper.
Three pages, each 11 x 8.5 inches

20 **Carving: A Traditional Sculpture**, 1972
Black and white photographs and text panel 144
photographs, each 7 x 5 inches
The Art Institute of Chicago, Twentieth Century
Discretionary Fund, 1996.

21 **The Eight Temptations**, 1972
Colour photographs, mounted on board
Eight photographs, each 7 x 5 inches

22 **The King**, 1972
Videotape (black and white, silent, fifty-two minutes)
Courtesy of Electronic Arts Intermix, New York

23 **Portraits of the King**, 1972
Black and white photographs, mounted on board
Three (of five) photographs, each 13.75 x 9.75 inches

24 Drawing from **The Kings's Meditations
(Banquet in the Clouds)**, 1974
Wash, ink, and chalk on photosensitive paper
13.5 x 17.5 inches. Lent by Marc Nochella, New York

25 Drawing from **The King's Meditations
(Country Cottage)**, 1974
Wash, ink and chalk on photosensitive paper
17.5 x 18.5 inches

26 **The King of Solana Beach**, 1974-75
Black and white photographs, mounted on board,
with text panels
Eleven photographs, two text panels, each 6 x 9 inches
Courtesy of The Washington University Gallery of Art,
St. Louis

27 **El Desdichado**, 1983
Videotape (colour, with sound, eight minutes); exerts of
video documentation of a live performance originally
staged at Ronald Feldman Fine Arts, New York

28 **The Adventures of a Nurse**
Video installation consisting of **The Adventures of a
Nurse**, 1976 videotape (colour, with sound, sixty-four
minutes); bed with bedspread and throw pillows; night
table; lamp; diary; and paper dolls
Dimensions variable
Videotape courtesy of Electronic Arts Intermix, New York

29 **The Nurse and the Hijackers** Video installation
consisting of **The Nurse and the Hijackers**, 1977
videotape (colour, with sound, sixty five minutes);
airplane set; and paper dolls
Dimensions variable
Sportscaster paper doll lent by Samuel David Winner,
M.D., Del Mar, California
Videotape courtesy of Electronic Arts Intermix, New York
Courtesy Dr. Winner

30 **Caught in the Act**, 1973
Video installation consisting of **Caught in the Act**, 1973,
videotape (black and white, with sound, thirty-six minutes)
Choreography I - Center Stage (Short Tutu), 1973
eight black and white photographs, mounted on board,
each 7 x 4 inches
Choreography II- Curtain Call (Long Tutu), 1973
seven black and white photographs, mounted on board,
each 7 x 4.75 inches
Choreography III - Classical Sighting (Long Tutu), 1973
six black and white photographs, mounted on board,
each 7 x 4.75 inches
Backstage Moments - Torn Ribbon, 1973
two black and white photographs, mounted on board,
each 7 x 4.75 inches
Backstage Moments - Making Up, 1973
black and white photograph, mounted on board,
7 x 4.75 inches
Backstage Moments - Waiting in the Wings, 1973
black an white photograph, mounted on board,
7 x 4.75 inches
Dimensions Variable
Videotape courtesy of Electronic Arts Intermix, New York

31 **The Ballerina and the Bum**, 1974
Videotape (black and white) fifty-four minutes
Courtesy of Electronic Arts Intermix, New York

32 **The little Match Girl Ballet**, 1975
Video tape (colour with sound) twenty seven minutes
Courtesy of Electronic Arts Intermix, New York

33 **Loves of a Ballerina**,
From **the Loves of a Ballerina**, 1986
Filmic installation, dressing table and props

34 **From the Archives of Modern Art**, 1987
Videotape (black and white) twenty-four minutes
Courtesy Milestone Film and video, New York

35 **The Last Night of Rasputin**, 1989
Videotape (black and white silent with music track) thirty-
eight minutes
Courtesy Milestone Film and video, New York

36 **The Man Without a World**, 1991
Videotape (black and white silent with music track)
ninety-eight minutes
Courtesy Milestone Film and video, New York

37 **Recollections of my Life with Diaghilev**, 1981
Handmade portfolios, Ballet slippers, 18 drawings,
lamp, potted palm and assorted objects.

Afterword

Arnolfini is pleased to be working with the Mead Gallery in presenting Britain's first exhibition of Eleanor Antin's groundbreaking work. Showing work by influential artists who are under-recognised in the UK is an important thread in Arnolfini's programming. Vito Acconci, Michael Snow, Gina Pane have - like Eleanor Antin - played vital roles in the contemporary art of Europe and North America. We are delighted to offer the opportunity for consideration of these artists, with the intention of stimulating artistic practice and critical discourse.

Caroline Collier **Catsou Roberts**
Director Senior Curator

Cornerhouse are proud to have worked together with the Mead Gallery and Arnolfini to present Eleanor Antin's first exhibition in the UK. Whilst Cornerhouse is primarily concerned with the presentation of new art, this show reiterates our commitment to the work of artists whose activities have led to a fundamental change in mentality towards contemporary art, its recognition, acceptance and appreciation.

Paul Bayley
Exhibitions Director

Acknowledgements

Many people have contributed to the development of this exhibition and its accompanying publication. In particular we would like to thank the Arts Council of England, Eleanor Antin, Electronic Arts Intermix, New York, Debby Freud, Angie Dugan at FAE, Petruta Lipan, Sabine Eckman, Ronald Feldman Fine Arts, New York, Howard N. Fox, Wayne Partridge and Angus McDonald at C'Art, Mainframe, Milestone Film and Video, New York.

Exhibition curated by Rachael Thomas and organised by Matt Golden and Sarah Shalgosky. Assisted by Lucy Anderson, Rachel Biddles, Kate O'Neil, Simon Martin, Caroline Smallwood, Eric Slater, Melanie Wood, Tamsin Wilkinson,

Catalogue design: David Bickerstaff

Lenders to Exhibition
Eleanor Antin
Ronald Feldman Fine Arts, New York
Marcia Goodman
Marc Nochella, New York
The Los Angeles County Museum of Art, Los Angles, California.
The Washington University Gallery of Art, Washington University. St Louis

Eleanor Antin: Real Time Streaming
A Mead Gallery Touring Exhibition supported by the Arts Council of England
Tel: +44 **(0)24 7652 4524**

Cornerhouse 3 March – 22 April 2001
70 Oxford Street, Manchester M1 5HN

The Arnolfini 18 March – 13 May 2001
16 Narrow Quay, Bristol, BS1 4QA

The Mead Gallery 6 October – 1 December 2001
Warwick Arts Centre, University of Warwick, Coventry CV4 7AL

ISBN 0 902683 52 7 - © 2001, the authors.

Cover image: Eleanor Antin,R.N. *The Adventures of a Nurse*, 1976
Videotape, colour, 64 min.
Courtesy Electronic Arts Intermix
Photo: Philip Steinmetz